ELEPHANT ON MY ROOF

WRITTEN AND ILLUSTRATED BY ERIN HARRIS

red
cygnet™
PRESS

San Diego, California

red
cygnet™
P R E S S

For my wonderful parents, and for Paulette and Micheal Faber,
who inspired this story. – E.H.

Illustrations copyright © 2007 Erin Harris
Manuscript copyright © 2007 Erin Harris
Book copyright © 2007 Red Cygnet Press, Inc., 11858 Stoney Peak Dr. #525, San Diego, CA 92128

Cover and book design: Amy Stirnkorb

First Edition 2007
10 9 8 7 6 5 4 3 2
Printed in China

Library of Congress Cataloging-in-Publication Data

Harris, Erin.
Elephant on my roof / written and illustrated by Erin Harris. -- 1st ed.
p. cm.
Summary: When Lani wakes up with an elephant on his roof and asks the villagers for help getting it down, their reluctance turns to enthusiasm when they discover that the elephant is a helpful addition to the community.
ISBN-13: 978-1-60108-002-8 (hardcover)
ISBN-10: 1-60108-002-6 (hardcover)
[1. Elephants--Fiction. 2. Community life--Fiction.] I. Title.
PZ7.H24126El 2007
[E]--dc22
2006017004

Lani found an elephant on his roof.

"How am I going to get the elephant down?" he asked himself.

Lani thought for a minute.

"Hmm... maybe he can jump
and I can catch him."

...Then he decided that perhaps it was not such a good idea.

Lani rowed into the village to ask for help.

"Absolutely not," said the fisherman. "He would get tangled in my net."

"An elephant running around town would be nothing but trouble."

"No way!" said
the children by
the coconut tree.

"I will not help,"
said the old woman.

"He would trample
my garden and make
such a big mess!"

It seemed as if nobody would help, but Lani would not give up.

"Please?" he begged.

"If the elephant causes any trouble, I will ask him to leave,"
said Lani.

The villagers grumbled to themselves but agreed.

The fisherman found an old boat...

...And the children gathered as much rope as they could.

They even took rope from the swings at the playground!

The next day, Lani and
the elephant rowed down the
river to thank everybody.

They came upon the fisherman first.

He was even grumpier than usual.

"Look at my net!" he said.

"It is so tangled that it will take me a week to fix it.

How am I going to catch fish now?"

Lani had an idea...

The fisherman thanked them.

Lani and the elephant waved goodbye and were on their way.

Next, they came upon the children.

"The coconuts are too high for us to reach!" they said.

"How will we get them down?"

Lani had an idea...

The children filled their arms with coconuts and Lani and the elephant continued on.

Soon they came upon the old lady.

"Look how many seeds
I have to plant!" she said.
"I cannot plant them
all by myself."

Lani had an idea...

The next day, as Lani and the elephant

were rowing down the river,

they came upon the fisherman again.

"Come with me," he said.
"I have another task for you."

It was a surprise party!

The townspeople brought fish,

coconuts, and mango juice to thank

Lani and the elephant for their help.

At the end of the day,

they waved goodbye to everybody.

"Come visit us any time,"

they said.

Lani and the elephant got back into their boat...

...and rowed home.